Shoeing the Fat

Real Women… Real Challenges… Real Talk!
A Mini-Style Guide

Photo by Yellock Images

By Shekina Moore

Shoeing the Fat
Real Women...Real Challenges... Real Talk!

By Shekina M. Moore
Entrepreneur. Designer. Stylist. Author.

"What good is it, my brothers, if a man claims to have faith but has no deeds? Can such faith save him? Suppose a brother or sister is without clothes and daily food. If one of you says to him, "Go, I wish you well; keep warm and well fed," but does nothing about his physical needs, what good is it? In the same way, faith by itself, if it is not accompanied by action, is dead."

James 2:14-17 (NIV)

Published by Around H.I.M. Publishing
For publishing information, address:

Around His Image Marketing and Publishing
PO Box 1373
Wake Forest, NC 27588
www.aroundHim.com

© 2011 by Shekina Moore
All Rights Reserved. Printed in the USA. No parts of this publication may be reproduced, translated, stored in any retrieval system or transmitted in any form or by electronic, mechanical, photocopying, recording or otherwise without the written permission of the author.

Literary Editor Sheila Hightower

Cover Design Tiana Davis

ISBN-13: 978-0615551241

Dedication

To my late Aunt Maggie Farr who gave me my first glimpse into my future when she shared *her closet* with me. To my mom who always taught me to smile to complete any outfit. To my father who always taught me the value of quality over quantity, and last but not least, to my husband who "gets it".

"You never know the degree to which simply being who you are will impact a generation."

Acknowledgements

There are so many talented individuals I would like to thank, not only for this book but for their support of my calling and gift. Thank you to my family Tommie L. Farr, Sr., Judy Wright Farr, Letonia Farr Page, Tommie Farr, Jr., and Cirita Farr, as well as the extended United Farr and Moore families, for your love, support and incessant prayers through this project and all I do. To my love, my husband, Stanford Moore; you have been on the frontlines as my biggest fan, sacrificing date nights and quality time to help me to see this project to fruition—thank you! To my son Colin, you are "mommy's angel" and you have such a sweet spirit. You provided me with all the love a mommy could ask for thank you! To Tiana Davis, thank you for your ability to translate my vision to the cover, making it what I could not articulate fully. You rock! To Ericka D. Jackson, Tonia Scott and TAG (Touch and Agree) Ministries, thank you from the bottom of my heart for your insight, guidance and belief in me. A warm thank you to Lauren Williams, Lisa Logroño, and Charity Fairley, for believing in my vision. Last, but certainly not least, thank you to Dr. Jeffrey Chapman, Sr., Sandie Chapman and my church family for your prayers and support. It was at Raleigh North Christian Center that I learned the art of *balance* and, most importantly began fully functioning in my gift.

Introduction

Stilettos. Heels. Peep-Toes. Wedges. Pumps. Just shoes! Give me shoes! Yes, shoes, shoes, shoes!

The silhouette alone can send a pulsing sensation up a woman's spine. Shoes are the consummate icon to the style-conscious. It is indelibly engrafted into our minds as we shop, as we pass women in the market place and on the streets. When we say "shoe" our minds instinctively go to a wonderful place, shoe heaven. I like that. So, as I engage you, let's "shoe" the fat, so to speak, in this style book addressing *real* women with *real* challenges through *real* talk.

Table of Contents

Dedication: iv

Acknowledgements: v

Introduction: vi

Chapter 1:   Who Are You? 9

Chapter 2:   Rid Yourself of Your Tolerations....17

Chapter 3:   Portions and Proportions.................27

Chapter 4:   Size (_) and Fabulous! 41

Chapter 5:   Personal Style 101 49

Chapter 6:   Style is Planned 59

Chapter 7:   A Tribute to French Swagger 71

Chapter 8:   Exclamation Points!!!........................79

Commentary: Divas Let Loose: 86

Call It A Cheat Sheet: 96

Biography: 111

Chapter 1: Who Are You?

"Perhaps you tend to avoid stepping outside of your comfort zone in an effort to just keep it safe. Doing that will only keep you away from fully developing your sense of style and it will result in feeling like your style is boring."

We are fearfully and wonderfully made. So why not you? The key to being charismatic is being present.

Shekina Moore

Yes, it would be wonderful to look like a 5′10″ gazelle in everything we wear, but the reality is, most of us are never going to look like that, regardless of how many pairs of shaping underwear we buy and no matter how few carbs we consume in a given day! You are never going to look like perfection all the time and the pursuit of perfection is such a waste of time. There are so many other things you could do with your time, not to mention your energy. So if you are wearing a dress that is maybe half an inch too short, but you feel great in it, wear it with confidence! If you feel confident, you will surely have a better time than the girl who looks perfect but lacks confidence.

Though you may have no intention of becoming like the people around you, if your mother is irritable and your best friend is homicidal & your boyfriend is a misogynist, you will unconsciously begin to manifest these behaviors before long. Be careful who you spend your time with. You must do the work while having the faith that the things you want will come. This means doing *something*. This does not mean waiting for things to come. You must get the ball rolling, get out in the water, get your feet wet; share, do the necessary research, do something. Move! Sheer faith in action will bring about creativity; appreciation will give you some perspective on your life and above all, you must remind yourself that there is a big, big world outside of your immediate surroundings.

Daily Tips

To help you style your way to success

This is a resource that includes some of my daily tips from my style blog from the past two years. I hope you find them helpful, resourceful and enjoyable.

"The right heels bring elegance to any outfit -- To ensure your feet aren't in pain all day, always be less conservative when choosing a size. Go up half a size to give your feet room to breathe, so you can walk hard in your pumps! "

"Less glam is more! Too often we are wearing too much glam in one outfit. Its messy and looks like we're trying too hard. An elegant look philosophy is this: pick one item to be your centerpiece to the outfit and everything else in the outfit is a compliment. Is it a splash of color in the shoes, glam earrings or chunky necklace? Pick one item to make your outfit unique yet sophisticated."

Nadia Shirin Moffett

Tips for Days 1-20:

Day 1:
There are many fab, color-rich, budget-conscious accessories for you to sink your fangs into. Do it! Your wardrobe will thank you for it and it costs little to make a big impact.

Day 2:
Ladies (frumpy moms & minimalists alike) there are 3 basics for a polished look for day: mascara, lipstick/stain/gloss, and blush/bronzer. Anything less says "I've given up!" That is not attractive, so, keep it tight!

Day 3:
A cheaper way to clean your makeup brushes is to use a dab of baby shampoo (old time favorite) and swirl only the bristles in your palm, rinse bristles only of all soap residue, reshape brush head & dry by resting on towel.

Day 4:
Old Man Winter got your skin looking ashy? Exfoliation is a must for brilliant skin, so, look to your kitchen to help you out! All you need is some sugar and water for your face (be very delicate now) and sea salt (a bit more abrasive) for your body. Add a few drops of lavender essential oil to your sea salt concoction and your body will be in relaxation heaven within a few strokes!

Day 5:
When it comes to RED, juicy lips follow this schemata:
- For yellow undertones-brown reds.
- For red undertones-blue reds.
- For blue undertones-plum reds.
- For red/orange undertones-orange reds.
- I highly recommend MAC's lip pencil in REDD. Hot lips rock!

Day 6:
After applying an eye shadow application to your lids, use a small eye shadow brush with a rounded tip to lightly dab a shimmery (think white, frosty pink or gold) shadow on the inner corners of the eyes. This will make them pop! This gives the "I'm wide awake" illusion!

Day 7:
Your handbag does not have to match your shoes (actually, its best they not match exactly -too contrived); it just needs to "go" with your shoes. Your choices should flow in some way... sheen, or texture, or pattern or style.

Day 8:
Never underestimate the importance of cleansing (as well as moisturizing) your face before you turn in. Sometimes you will be tempted to cheat after a long night. Just in case, keep facial wipes handy for speedy cleansing to combat the naughty temptation. Failure to cleanse after a while will enlarge your pores (a.k.a. AGING). And who wants that? That will surely come,

in time. But who says we can't prolong it! So come on, let's hold it back.

Day 9:
Need a lift? Extend your brows outward, not downward to give your face a lift. Downward does you no service.

Day 10:
Neutrals never go out of style!

Day 11:
When you leave the house make sure your undergarments are special. It will give you an unwavering confidence and strut. If your undergarments need an overhaul, make the decision to get rid of the granny panties today.

Day 12:
When it comes to wedding makeup, do not take the coin "natural beauty" literally. Seeking a professional makeup artist is quintessential to a polished finish... yielding bridal face shots to savor for years to come.

Day 13:
Jewelry can make all the difference in your wardrobe. It makes the simple special.

Day 14:
OK, OK, OK.... Look, you can't even think about makeup until your skin is in order! For healthy skin, we know to cleanse and moisturize, exfoliate and use SPF. However, did you know the benefit of detoxing?

Detoxing rids your body of impurities that manifest in your SKIN!

Day 15:
It doesn't have to match, it just has to "go". Too much matching is a *faux pas*.

Day 16:
My makeup case contains:
Waterproof mascara! If you are going to a tear-jerking event, please, please, please make sure you wear waterproof mascara! Otherwise, you may end up looking like you just came out of a bout with "Who Shot John?" I am personally partial to Chanel's waterproof mascara.

Day 17:
Orange Lips! The look is absolutely fabulous. The energy and attractiveness given off by orange lips is amazing!

Day 18:
Bored with your hair but don't want a cut? Need a change? Highlights! Remember to use a conditioning glaze if you color your hair.

Day 19:
Drinking water is essential for nice, glowing skin. Don't like to drink water? Make drinking water a treat by putting FUN in water. Pour water into a nice wine glass and embellish the glass with berries and citrus fruits. After all, color stimulates the senses. ...And the look is simply DIVA!

Day 20:

Closet Organization will save you TIME and MONEY! So, let's get to it! Sort, Purge, Assess, Containerize and Equalize!

Chapter 2: Rid Yourself of Your Tolerations

"At the end of each dry hot summer day, HYDRATE your skin. Use a soft facial cleanser, follow up with a toner, apply a serum designed for your skin type, and finish with a night moisturizer to wake up refreshed and renewed."

"S.T.Y.L.E. (Show That You Live Excellence) Your style should reflect your personal brand. Accessories are the best tools to accentuate your style. Whether it's a flower in your hair or on your lapel, be bold and be elegant. Most importantly, be YOU."

Marshawn Evans

I was attending a conference in which a millionaire was the keynote speaker. Two things from that conference really stood out, the incredibly delicious meal we feasted upon and a quote the keynote speaker used: "Get rid of your tolerations!"

Rid yourself of your tolerations? I thought, "What does that mean?" She went on to explain that our tolerations cost us dearly. They cost us time, energy, money and opportunities. In an instant, this forced me to reflect on my life, my routines, my habits, my tolerations. Ultimately, they were delaying me and I realized I ran the risk of sabotaging my destiny.

Tolerations come in all packages, especially for women:

- Saying yes to others when it means saying no to ourselves ("Yes-ing").
- Trying to do too many things at once, provoking anxiety, raising blood pressure ("Multi-tasking").
- Thinking we have to do it all and feeling like we dropped the ball when we really can't do it all ("Feeling Guilty").
- Over-consumption of caffeine to get that pick-me-up, in an effort to do it all ("Morning Coffee").

The toleration I want to focus on for the sake of this book is the over-crowded closet. I had not given much thought to this toleration prior to the keynote speaker's commentary, but my eyes were now wide open as if she were looking directly at me and could peep into my closet. My closet was severely overstuffed to such a degree that I was reduced to stepping over this to get to that. I admit to falling in my closet on a few occasions; however, I had finally mastered which steps to take to avoid falls. I had learned to tolerate the inconvenience of this overflowing, messy closet with all sorts of outlandish reasoning's:

- "I might wear that again one day."
- "I plan to lose weight."
- "I paid too much for that one."
- "Just in case I gain weight again."
- "I can't wear the same thing in the same month! If I get rid of all of my stuff, what will I wear?"
- "This is coming back in style." And so on.

The truth of the matter is searching in a messy closet or poking through a dresser bursting with pieces you no longer can wear adds undue stress to your morning. I ask you, who needs more stress? Really! So, if like me you find you are head-over-heels in "tolerations" like this one, the good news is you don't have to be.

Four times a year put everything into one of these piles and rid yourself of them!

1. Trash – irreparable/badly stained/no use to anyone.
2. Donations – these are the items that don't fit you now and you are not sentimental enough to give to a loved one.
3. Cleaning – you would wear it tomorrow if it did not need to be cleaned, dry cleaned or mended.

4. Storage – you are 100% excited about wearing it next season.

Suggestion: With everything that's in you, try not to make excuses and deviate from the process.

Ultimately, once your closet is clean and de-cluttered, items are easily accessed, and you can actually fit all you reach for, you will feel less anxiety and less stress; and most assuredly, to make mention, you will save yourself time and energy. Best of all, you will look and feel GREAT!

Tips for Days 21-41:

Day 21:
Under-eye "shadows" often are created by falling eye shadow residue during application. To alleviate this problem place a square of tissue directly under your eye while you apply your shadow with a BRUSH.

Day 22:
Say no to blackheads! Blackheads are annoying little unsightly spots on the face and other areas of the skin where oil has built up and become trapped inside the pore. Blackhead extractors are instruments used by professional beauty therapists to gently lever out blockages and blackheads from the skin. An extractor is basically a stainless steel tool with a scoop-shaped end with a central hole. You don't have to visit a professional to have your blackheads removed. You can get rid of them yourself, at home, with a blackhead extractor. Visit Sephora!

Day 23:
Ladies! Always be ready! Pack your BEAUTY SURVIVAL KIT and put it in your trunk!
It should include: clear lip gloss/chap stick, floss/toothpicks, mini mouthwash, mini perfume spritzer, hairspray/gel, mini bottle of lotion, tissues, Visine, clear nail polish, nude pantyhose, mini toothpaste & toothbrush.

Day 24:
If your nails are stained from dark polish, stick your fingers into lemon halves for five minutes—it's an instant brightener.

Day 25:
For my clients who have unsightly tattoos they want to cover for special events, I use my trusted She LaQ over my concealer! The She LaQ is fabulous and is sold at Benefit Cosmetics. I promise you…it won't rub off on anyone!

Hint: It can also be mixed with water and mist-sprayed over your face to hold your makeup in place. It defies rain, humidity, and tears. How yum is that!

Day 26:
Trade up your cheap nick-knacks (bad habit) for QUALITY pieces!!!
If you are over the age of 30 it is about time you invested in QUALITY sunglasses that make you feel and look GREAT the instant you glide them on! Visit Saks 5th Avenue's Kiosk... sunglass heaven!

Day 27:
The skinny on a basic smoky eye:
[To create a gorgeous night-time look] Use light, medium and dark eye shadow shades in graduated tones. Apply the dark shade along your lash line, the medium shade on the crease, and a light shade up to the eyebrow bone but not beyond. Soften and BLEND any hard edges so that each color seems to melt into the next.

Day 28: Have a man?
Men, come on, of course your shoes need to be quality and well-maintained: Clean and polished. At hello, we are looking down at your feet and sizing you up. Besides, a woman's eagle eye can spot cheap shoes a mile away.

Day 29: Have a man?
To add length, shorter men should invest in suits with 3 or more buttons. Taller men should wear 3 buttons or less to lend balance.

Day 30:
Pink in a sophisticated shade is universally flattering. Aim somewhere between light pink and peach. Neutral is at its best. Eggplant is another great universal flattering hue. It's "the perfect purple" because it is extremely versatile, almost like a black, a dark brown, or a navy. Rock it!

Day 31:
From the perspective of Feng Shui, our homes mirror our inner lives, and everything in our homes says something about us on a psychological level. Our belongings have symbolic meanings as well as obvious ones. How we utilize, display, and care for our property reveals how we feel about ourselves and our lives. What does your home say about you? Hmmm....

Day 32:
NO MORE WIRE HANGERS...EVER! I know the cleaners gave them to you, but throw them out! They make creases in your garments. Worse, they can rust

and leave stains on clothing. Switch to wood, plastic or padded fabric hangers to protect your good clothes and keep them looking their best.

Day 33:
Your hairstyle MUST flatter your face shape and features.

Day 34:
If you, like me, have finally resolved to shape up your body in prep for next summer attire, take a few hours to prepare your meals for the week. Exercise is a MUST. Begin to walk and detox once a week for at least the first 30 days.

Day 35:
When it comes to spring cleaning, it's not about what you don't WANT or don't NEED. It's about what you don't USE and what you don't WEAR! Huge distinction. "Garage Sale" is calling your name.

Day 36:
Avoid wedding day shoe blues. Break in your new pair before the wedding day. Walk, dance in them two weeks prior to your big day! Also, if you have a shoe fetish, let it show on your wedding day! Don't be shy!

Day 37:
Wear a romper as a cover-up at the pool or beach. They come in all colors and patterns. Add flip-flops or gladiator sandals and you are ready.

Day 38:
Reserve waterproof mascara for "special" occasions as regular use is harsh and can be damaging to the lashes. Using translucent powder can effectively highlight your lashes without daily mascara use.

Day 39:
Do not wear out your bras by wearing them back to back. Instead rotate them so that the will maintain their elasticity. Also, invest in a black and nude strapless. Avoid white strapless' as they get dingy ...fast.

Day 40:
Beige never looks good near the face so break it up with a turquoise necklace or a bright cardigan. Somehow, make the beige pop or standout!

Day 41:
Hairy upper lips don't have to be waxed. Try "Jolen's Creme Bleach" to blend excess hair on face, arms & body with your own skin tones. Just lighten up for a flawless look!

Chapter 3: Portions and Proportions

"Nothing says power & confidence like a signature color. Find the hue that brings your spirit to life and work it!"

Tanea Smith

Show me a put-together woman and I will show you a line of men with their tongues wagging. That's right. So, what is it about the put-together woman that sends the message to other women that they better step up their game?

The answer is simple. People are attracted to, and, yes, want to be around *style*! Style says so much about who you are! Like it or not, leave it or take it, your style is reflecting something to all with whom you come in contact. The sheer essence of you is being illuminated as you go to and fro conducting business, frequenting the salon, mentoring, dinging with friends, sashaying across campus, even shopping for groceries. Before a stranger ever says 'hello' he is absorbing the essence of who you are. I regularly come across women who are powerful in their own right, true forces to be reckoned with, who contribute greatly to their communities and society at large. Yet there is an element missing; or perhaps gone awry. As obvious as an elephant in a room, that no one dares to mention, I speak of the element of *style*. It is amazing that you can be the best at whatever it is you do and people will still be distracted by your lack of style sense.

Have you ever met this woman? She is so gifted, so talented, so incredibly dynamic, *BUT*... It is this very "*BUT*..." that inspired me to write this book. Successful women around the globe are in a rut and, sadly, some do not even realize it. Meanwhile, everyone around them is praying that prayer. You know the one... "Lord, if only they had some style." We all know her. She is our best friend, our co-worker, our committee member, our kid's teacher, our sister, our attorney, our aunt, our mother, our high school classmate, our neighbor, our first lady, our professor, our news anchor etc... She is in the aisles at the grocery store. She's even in front of large audiences. She is so busy saving the world or taking care of others or pursuing her dreams that she either has not noticed or has decided it simply is not a priority.

It's about *knowing* what looks good on you. It's about playing up your best assets and disguising the ones you don't feel confident about. If you want to look good you have to look at yourself in the mirror - objectively inspect the contours, shape, proportions and color of your body. Improving your style is part of the self-development process that helps you achieve a sense of confidence and comfort in the person you are. Often this self-acceptance or self-development will radiate through the way you dress and you will attract the same admirations style icons like Audrey Hepburn and Marilyn Monroe still garner today.

Their strategy? Well, they knew that they didn't need to have a "certain look" to look good. Instead, they accentuated their individuality.

Marilyn Monroe had the curves and personality to create that feminine, sexy image for which she was well known. Imagine if we put her signature halter dress on slim-trim sporty and sophisticated Audrey Hepburn...uh-uh, big mistake! That would emphasize her thin arms and enhance her boyish shape. Imagine how out of place she would feel! Audrey's straight, minimal tee shirt and pants on Marilyn......don't get me started! See why some trends and clothing styles you see in magazines (albeit, beautiful and gorgeous as they are) are just not for some people –in fact, they just don't look good on them.

Silhouettes ride on the fit. It is all about the clean line. Anytime you see puckers in your waist, *stop*! The line has been broken. I often recommend clients to sit in the dressing room to see if they can sit comfortably in a garment and to test if there is too much stretch or bunching. Mastering the ideal silhouette means becoming very familiar with your core/body shape. There are four basic body shapes:

<u>The Candy Apple</u>
You carry most of your weight in your midsection. This can make you look wider and shorter if your proportions are not counteracted. So, the goal is to minimize your middle and place emphasis on those gorgeous gams of yours.

Must-haves:
- Single-button blazers
- A-line shifts
- Short skirts
- Wide-leg trousers
- Bold-colored bottoms
- Printed skirts
- Wrap dresses and shirts
- Long necklaces
- Shirts that fall to the hips
- V-necks, scoop necks, cowl necks
- Trouser-cut jeans with straight leg

Avoid:
- Blouses with bold patterns
- Chunky knits
- Shoulder pads
- Shiny fabrics
- Tapered pants
- Short jackets that hit at the waist
- Low-rise jeans

The Sweet Pear

You store most of your weight below the waist. Your hips are fuller and your shoulders are narrow with a small bust and midsection. The goal is to draw the eye away from your broadest point (your hips) and to balance your arms and shoulders.

Must-haves:
- A-line skirts
- Bright shirts
- Printed shirts, patterned blouses
- Turtle necks
- Blazers
- Puffed sleeves
- Jackets that hit at the waist or mid-thigh
- Flat-front pants with wide leg that skims the hips
- Shirts with ruching
- Boot-cut jeans with large pockets on backside

Avoid:
- Light-colored pants
- Patterned pants
- Bias-cut dresses
- Straight skirts
- Cargo pants
- Pants with lots of pockets

The Rocking Ruler

You have an athletic build and a straight up and down figure with fewer curves. You share the shape of most runway models and have your choice of clothing options. The goal is to add some contour and a feminine touch to your silhouette by accentuating your waist.

Must-haves:
- Wide and skinny belts
- Ruffles
- Pleats
- Floral design clothing
- Bias-cut jackets
- Pencil skirts
- Flare-cut skirts
- Jackets with darts at the waist
- A padded bra
- Low-rise jeans with embellished pockets
- High-waist trousers
- Skinny jeans

Avoid:
- Vertical lines
- Short tops and jackets

The Timeless Hourglass
You have symmetrical curves with an emphasis on hip to bust ratio. Your narrow waist takes much credit in creating the appealing silhouette. Therefore, the goal here is to show off your waist.

Must-haves:
- High-waist pants
- Belted coats and jackets
- Pocket-less pants
- Boot-cut bottoms
- Flared bottoms
- Wrap tops that hit at the waist

- Light-knit cardigans
- Wrap dresses
- Jeans with some lycra (stretch)

Avoid
- Trapeze dresses or shifts
- Skirts/dresses that gather at the hips

Tips for Days 42-62:

Day 42:
POLKA DOTS! A word to the wise, if you choose to go for this graphic look, consider your size. Don't pick a pattern that will overwhelm your look. For example, petite women should opt for small to medium polka dots while voluptuous ladies should feel free to experiment with bolder pieces.

Day 43:
Did you know that even skin tone (just as white teeth) makes you look younger? Chances are if you don't exfoliate daily or weekly, your skin is covered in dead skin cells that are mucking up the surface of your skin and causing your skin to not only look dull, but older as well. Without proper exfoliation your foundation will not smooth over your cleaned skin and your moisturizer will not properly soak in.

Day 44:
Transform your spring/summer dresses to fall by layering a crew-neck sweater or cardigan on top, adding a skinny belt, and trading up your sandals for pumps or booties.

Day 45:
The bigger the handbag, the smaller your butt looks! The smaller the handbag...

Day 46:
Coordinate, don't match. Coordinate, don't match. Coordinate, don't match. You get it!

Day 47:
Have a signature. What's your signature? What statement do you make via your personal style? Your personal style should be known. Mine is my short, sleek hair and my sideburns even... so when I deviate, people comment and take notice. That's a good thing. What's yours?

Day 48:
Your feet swell throughout the day. Be sure to buy shoes at the END of the day to avoid buyer's regret.

Day 49:
Pay the money and get a color analysis. It makes no sense to continue to buy hues that do not suit your skin tone.

Day 50:
Next Spring will be here before we know it. Make sure you add 2 teaspoons of sugar and a dollop of baby oil to your shower gel bottle of choice. Shake, shake, shake... and please do USE for skin that glistens and screams, "I take care of myself"!

Day 51:
Avoid VPL (visible panty lines) at all costs. It is unsightly. Really! Say it with me... NO MORE VPL, NO MORE VPL, NO MORE VPL!!! Seriously, if your panties are shifting in any way, the whole world will know it.

Day 52:
When it comes to traditional lash curlers, your lashes will curl when you pump (open-close, open-close, and open-close) the curler. Note, this motion forms the curl, so clamping down real tight and holding is a common mistake. Only use it BEFORE you apply your mascara so you won't pull out your lashes (yikes!) ...unless you are using a heated lash curler, which is a totally different ball game altogether.

Day 53:
Does your lipstick bleed, leaving lipstick running up the fine lines of your mouth? Not cute, right? Well, Too Faced's Lip Insurance lip primer (sold at Ulta & Sephora) is just the ticket! Use it as a base to prevent lipstick creasing and bleeding; in this way you can keep it hot!

Day 54:
A lesson on brushes: Natural vs. Synthetic Bristles
Natural bristles are very soft and offer a more blended, natural application. They are best for all powders, blushes and shadows. In contrast, synthetic bristles are stiffer so they will give you greater control and precision. They are best for creamy products like concealers, lip colors, gel liners, etc.

Day 55:
No one is finished unless they smell good. Don't save perfume for special occasions. Take note now....apply perfume lightly to the body's pulse points: the wrists, base of the throat, behind the ear lobes, the bend in

your elbows, and between the breasts. The secret agent word being *lightly*.

Day 56:
Lashes seem like such a small detail, huh? But for the woman who loves to bat her thinning lashes can be unnerving. Well... lashes, like the hair on our heads, need conditioning. Eyelashes tend to get dry and brittle from cosmetics and other environmental factors. If your lashes are not conditioned regularly, they will begin to flake and eventually fall out, irritating the eyes in the process. Using a lash conditioner will keep your lashes supple and able to handle the cosmetics and other stresses they encounter. You heard it straight from S.O.!

Day 57:
You ARE what you EAT. Just take a picture of your refrigerator. Journal your meals; in fact, take inventory of what you are eating. It bears to be repeated....you ARE what you EAT. Health and beauty go hand in hand. Don't feed one and starve the other. Think "balance".

Day 58:
Do your consumer research. Don't just buy from anyone.

Day 59:
Crowded closets mean wrinkled clothes. Bless someone with clothes you have not worn in a year or more. *Less* truly is *more*.

Day 60:
For costume parties, Halloween parties or dress-up you can cover your brows and redraw them with Dermablend and follow with She LaQ and powder... You will look totally different! Seek me out when you are ready!

Day 61:
It's fun to play with makeup. The trick is knowing when and where to stop.

Day 62:
When transforming a day face to an evening face, start with a touch of eye cream to smooth out existing concealer. Then, reapply concealer as needed.

Chapter 4: Size (_) and Fabulous!

"Consider ways you can incorporate your brand into wardrobe -- with your logo, a recognizable piece of jewelry, or a specific color. For years I was known as the "Paper Tiger Lady" and my wardrobe was full of tiger stripes which was fun and memorable for my clients!"

Barbara Hemphill

Let's face it. It's hard to feel fabulous if your self-esteem suffers from poor body image. No matter your number on the scale and no matter your size of dress get over the number and feast your eyes on your ASSETS! Yes, we all have them, glorious ASSETS! Think on your best asset. Is it your dimples? Your ankles? Your hair? Your cheekbones? Your legs? Your shape? Your waistline? Yes, think happy thoughts when naked, no negative energy allowed.

Stuck? Can't pin point your best asset? Pay attention to what you are most complimented on. Once you have a clue that "you have it going on", accentuate it! If your face is your shining glory, keep your neckline open to draw the eye upward directly to your face. Nice behind? A pencil skirt will surely garner your back side the attention it deserves, and if legs could kill, yours would be in cigarette pants, skinny jeans and short skirts.

The fact is many of us find it hard to stand in front of a mirror and find something to like about our bodies. It's much easier to point out every flaw, either real or perceived, than to find something we love about our bodies. The sad part is that even when we have someone in our lives who loves us for who we are, many of us have difficulty fully accepting it.

Out of proportion? Riddled with cellulite? Flabby arms? Stretch marks? Tree trunk thighs? Chubby knees? Blemishes? Short neck? Join the club! Who cares! Who is looking for perfection? In fact, perfection is a fantasy. In the real world it is what it is. Did you know that "Real" is sexy. Cookie cutter is not. Learn the art of being happy in your own skin.

Women come in all shapes and sizes, and we possess the tools to help us find the best style to compliment our assets. Think about it. Curvy brides have choices now –they really do. They are no longer relegated to the back of the bridal (fashion) bus or to the all purpose A-line silhouette. Designers and bridal manufacturers have finally realized that being in the plus size does not equate to being shaped like a slab of meat.

Plus size or not, what it all boils down to is *confidence*. Your level of self-confidence can be revealed in many ways: *via* your behavior, your body language, how you speak, what you say, and so on. Two main things contribute to self-confidence: *self-efficacy* and *self-esteem*. We gain a sense of self-efficacy (the confidence that, if we learn and work hard in a particular area, we will succeed) and self-esteem (which comes from the sense that if we are behaving virtuously, we are competent at what we do, and we can compete successfully when we put our minds to it).

It is therefore vital that we think about where we are going, set goals, and shut down negative self-talk that creates the images of doom in our minds. If this book is in your hands you have already taken the first step needed to move in the right direction concerning your body image. You are, after all, thinking about where you are going. Kudos to you!

Tips for Days 63-83:

Day 63:
To make your nose look smaller – apply blush closer to your nose.

Day 64:
Losing elasticity in your skin? Try Aveeno Ageless Vitality. The product is shown to build blocks of elastin which improves firmness, wrinkles, brown spots and texture.

Day 65:
Got wrinkles? Try StriVectin, an instant deep wrinkle filler that reduces the appearance of fine lines and wrinkles. Sold at Bloomingdale's, Saks, Macy's, Sephora and Ulta.

Day 66:
Mascara makes your eyes look full of energy, so give those limp lashes a boost and shun (at all costs) skipping this important step. To the shy ladies, use a classic brown or clear. :-)

Day 67:
Why not sport an ultra-feminine frock to your next event. Think Chantilly lace dress, ruffle and pearl detail, embroidered silk plisse dress, embroidered tulle, knotted and woven ribbon detail, lace, ostrich feather and silk organza dress. It's all in the details.

Day 68:
If it's the first time you're seeing a stylist, dress up a little. This allows a stylist to get a sense of your personal style, so he/she can give you a cut that works with your personal style. Now please, don't roll up to the salon looking like *who shot john*.

Day 69:
If your hair is flat at the root and consequently limp... use a root lifter/booster. Great for fine hair babes!

Day 70:
Spa day is worth the splurge. It inspires you to slow down and restore yourself. A peaceful oasis. It is an essential element of beauty and wellness.
P.S. Brides should get a facial at least four days prior to the wedding. Any day closer than that is a major no-no.

Day 71:
I know you traditionally save your brooches for fall and winter to accompany your coats & scarves, right? Well, why not use them now and be cleverly cute? Rock one on your thin belts layered over a summer dress... or on your purse for added panache, or even on your headband to surely turn heads... so very chic.

Day 72:
OK, your wardrobe needs work. Start by ridding yourself of every outfit you simply do not feel good in. Let's see, you've been storing that outfit up for what.... the past five years? Life's too short to be waiting to lose those last 10 pounds.

Day 73:
Always wanted to try colored mascara but never got around to buying it? Dip the 205 Mascara Fan Brush into any eye shadow (frosts work best) and sweep it onto your lashes while your mascara is still wet. Now you don't have to spend extra money on colored mascara!

Day 74:
Give the clothes you already have a boost. This only requires thinking outside the box. Have hemlines you wish were just an inch longer? Add a different fabric or a ruffle to a too-short hemline. Re-line a blazer with a contrasting color or pattern, then roll your sleeves 3/4 length to show it off! Chop a tired log skirt into a mini. Change the buttons on a tired blouse.... And voila!
Read: ~The Shopping Diet by Phillip Bloch~

Day 75:
Being beautiful includes healthy living. Beauty can be seen as feeling great, so, annually schedule your pelvic and breast exams appropriately. From the physical aspect, this includes heart exams, thyroid tests, blood glucose, heart listen, blood pressure, cholesterol reading at age 35; mammograms at 40; rectal exam, lymph nose exam, lung exam, and measuring size of internal organs for enlargement at 40; colonoscopy at 45 (not 50).

Day 76:
Consider bringing your own nail file to the salon on your next visit since nail files cannot be sterilized. Be

proactive and alert; these are things that make you say hmmm....

Day 77:
Getting married next year? Bold lips are making a serious comeback! I'm loving it! Can't you tell!

Day 78:
If you are challenged with dry skin....try L'Occitane. If you are Vegan, try L'Occitane, and, if you have skin allergies... L'Occitane. Great stuff!

Day 79:
Use a bronzer over tinted moisturizer to give your skin a beautiful, natural summer glow. Hint: Cut your foundation with an SPF moisturizer for homemade tinted moisturizer. This is much lighter -more sheer- for hot seasons AND will save you money.

Day 80:
Never pop or touch pimples. Your hands can transfer more breakout-inducing bacteria to the area. Besides, most of us squeeze too hard, causing trauma to the skin, causing a pip-squeak pimple to turn into a huge, inflamed cyst. Rather, use an anti-inflammatory cortisone cream 2x a day. Follow with benzyl peroxide or salicylic acid.

Day 81:
Don a maxi skirt. A fitted one will make you look long and lean, while a loose one has a more casual and fun feel. You can wear a tank top with it or a nice blouse.

Day 82:
The shrunken denim jacket is back in full effect. So is the roomy, non-structured clutch for DAY! So incredibly chic!

Day 83:
Spring is the best time to buy for Fall. I bet you are ready to say boots! Finds from last season are on the racks now... on SALE. Don't believe me? Stop by Nordstrom. Looka there! I just saw your eyes get big.

Chapter 5: Personal Style 101

"Create a tinted moisturizer for sheer coverage by mixing your foundation with a sunscreen or your favorite moisturizer."

"Maintain a groomed eyebrow to elevate your look."

Denise Tunnell

I love this topic because I know the impact it has on the lives of women across the globe. So many people make the mistake of confusing style for fashion. Yet they could not be more different. Bridgette West, publisher of Charlotte Style Magazine, frames it perfectly: "Fashion is dictated, Style is personal."

Imagine picking out special songs for your wedding day CD. You wouldn't pick anything that did not reflect who you are, right? Why? Because you would want to put your personal stamp on your special CD in such a way that every time a song is played, your mind goes to that place. This place is yours, your magic/your essence. Then later, you realize (as will others) at various events like your anniversaries, parties with your friends, the songs come on the radio and your eyes sparkle, that sparkle says, "that's *our* song!" Each song you selected is your signature song. You stake claim to it. You profess it. You own it.

Personal style works in much the same way. Your style is your very own rendition of you. Therefore, we do not mimic it; we feel it, we *own* it as *signature*. Brigitte Bardot wore her signature cat eye makeup and it was as distinctive as signing her name.

All fashion does not fit your size, personality, lifestyle, age, or character. There are countless interpretations of style but the one that counts is the one you give the world when the sun kisses your face each day. Perhaps you have admired someone else's own personal sense of style, but you have been too shy or too busy to place much attention on your personal style. This style is what makes you...*you* and makes you unique. It's your time to claim your personal style.

Two women can be at the same event, donning the same basic black cocktail dress. It is their personal style that will shine through. One may be classic and choose to pair the dress with classic, black peep-toe pumps, bangles and a blazer. The other may finish her look with a fabulous pair of stilettos, accessorized with a chunky statement necklace that proclaims, "I have arrived!"

Caution! What makes lady #1 feel distinctive and confident may not make lady #2 feel so great and vice versa. The goal is to find the right clothes that will fit your body, as well as the clothes that will go from season to season so that you can build on your wardrobe staples with items that make you, well, *you*.

Classics go with all personal styles. The decision-making moment is when you are faced with TRENDS! Yes, trends. The most popular jean silhouette on the market may not necessarily look best on your figure. The oversized ethnic necklace may be "all the rave" and may actually be cute on her but may not match your personality… not to mention your head size or petite frame.

Invest in key pieces you love. Your wardrobe does not need to be huge. It only needs to be special and make you feel great. So, personal style comes from knowing your body type and knowing what looks good on you, including color. Balance trends, but stay true to yourself.

Always begin by layering the first piece- usually something classic from your closet such as a LBD (Little Black Dress), a black pencil skirt, dark jeans, a crisp white shirt, etc. Consider layering pieces that add texture and dimension.

When we invest in exceptionally well-made classic pieces that we will wear over and over again, we can stay on trend without being trendy. You can incorporate trends to your style by using smaller pieces (accessories) that you do not have to spend a lot for and all the while, make it easy to change up your look. Scarves, necklaces, earrings, watches, bangles do the trick.

Again, a signature piece is an item or style that identifies you almost like a fashion I.D. card. This is becoming increasingly important when building your style because it separates you from the rest. Your signature piece can be glamorous oversized sunglasses or different scarves worn practically every day -- anything that adds originality to your look. It's perfectly fine to splurge on these pieces because they represent you and help define your style, plus, you'll get multiple wear and outfits out of them.

The next time you are out and about shopping or raking the racks online, ask yourself some questions: Who am I? Will the clothing style reflect my personality? Will it be classy? Will it be eclectic? How about sporty? Laid back? Trendy? Sophisticated? Will the item make me feel great? Will the design(s) bring out the parts you like about yourself? -- Great legs? Pretty face? Super nice hair? Feminine waist? etc., etc.

In developing your personal style it is best to avoid wearing just one designer style head to toe --and never become a slave to it. Mix it up! And by all means, remember this one rule and say it with me: *Just because "everyone's wearing it" does not mean I must join the club.*

Tips for Days 84-103:

Day 84:
Make sure your bra FITS. You're 35. The bra you wore at 20 should no longer be in your chest of drawers.

Day 85:
If your teeth are DULL, beige/yellow or even brown ….. Go have them WHITENED! It makes you look younger and more polished. Dull teeth say "I need maintenance." Sorry, but it does.

Day 86:
Buy at least one new statement piece whenever you go somewhere. Once you're home, it's a reminder of the place you've been and always a treasure to wear because it has a story behind it.

Day 87:
Looks like BIG HAIR is shaping up for the Fall and Winter. So, if you've got it, flaunt it! Just don't hit me with it and we'll be alright.

Day 88:
NEVER let your hair get in the way of your workout. You will always be very glad that you worked your body. You want to LOOK good and FEEL good too. You Go Girl!

Day 89:
You will always look like a million bucks when you invest in your accessories. Bags are statement pieces. I picked up the Coach Drawstring bag (reminiscent of

the 70s) and love it. It's so roomy because of its shape, yet arm candy that does not weigh me down. Check out this season's looks. Looks like the "Lady Bag" is also back! It's perfect for the business suit, tea time and Sundays.

Day 90:
Did you know? Cap sleeves can make your arms look heavier; scoop necks that add even more roundness up top to well-endowed women; pants that taper to the ankle create an upside-down pyramid; pleated pants add bunched up fabric where you want it least; ankle-strap shoes cut across your legs, stopping the eyes and making the leg look chunky; and vertical stripes ripple, creating unattractive curvy lines on your body.

Hint: Wrap dresses and plunging necklines make you look thinner.

Day 91:
Invest in a nice, classic red lipstick. It is the go-to pout that NEVER goes out of style.

Day 92:
When it comes to jackets, there's one golden rule: Don't scrimp! The jacket is often the first thing people see when you arrive and the last thing they see when you leave. So, invest in a great coat that not only looks wonderful and fits well but also keeps you warm. If you prefer classics, you can't go wrong with a trench or wool pea coat in camel or navy.

Day 93:
Create the image you want. Think about where you are going, forget about where you are. Need help? Give me a call or book an appointment. My contact info is as follows: www.ShekinaMoore.com

Day 94:
Wear metallics to spice up an outfit. Pair up silver shoes with a romper to add flair to a date-night outfit. Wear a gold tote for an everyday look. If that's too much, you can always just paint your nails a metallic shade.

Day 95:
Keep a compact and a tube of lipstick in your purse or desk for emergencies at work. You don't really need anything else for quick touch-ups. Keep it fresh and more natural for work a la Kate Bosworth.

Day 96:
Don't try to be anyone else. Be the BEST YOU, *you* can be. Haters will be haters.

Day 97:
Help your lip color last by blending your foundation over your lip line and lips so short-lived gloss and sheer lipsticks have something to grab on to. Fill in lips with a neutral lip pencil. Blot lips. After applying lipstick, hold a Kleenex over your lips and brush on translucent powder. This will sift through and set the makeup.

Day 98:
Don't obsess over size! First of all, being petite or plus-sized has nothing-- zip! zilch! zero!-- to do with how beautiful you are. Secondly, almost every designer these days uses a different sizing chart. You may be a 6 in one designer and a 10 in another. Buy what fits well and you'll FEEL gorgeous. Once you get home tear out the size tag!

Day 99:
Instead of buying a new $100 dress I decided to take 5 of my favorite dresses from my wardrobe to the tailor this morning. Next time you want to treat yourself, consider taking 5 items from your closet to a tailor. Tailored clothes look more expensive because they look (and, in fact, are) custom fit. Besides, it feels really good to have inches taken in!

Day 100:
Like makeup, perfume allows you to express yourself without saying a word. In addition to sending a message to others it affects your mood. Peppermint can distract you from pain. Lavender can make you feel relaxed. But do be careful when you spritz the wrists--touch together--don't rub. Rubbing alters the fragrance.

Day 101:
Find your go-to fragrance. If you smell good, you feel good. It is also a way to express yourself. Here are the go-to fragrances for the SoKina team. Shekina Moore and Lauren Ashley like Vera Wang. Charity Fairley

wears Chance by Chanel and Lisa Logrono adores Miss Dior Cherie.

Day 102:
The crisp white shirt –you know the one that buttons down the front (no button-down collar, no pockets) can be dressed up or down. Seriously, what else looks equally great over a bathing suit, with jeans and under a business suit!

Day 103:
It is perfectly ok to have a chipped nail polish day, a bad hair day, a missing button on my sweater day, even a too much makeup day. Just don't make it a habit (e.g., bad hair week, ashy elbow month) and please, don't have them all in the same day (i.e., a hot mess).

Continue on being human; nobody is perfect. After all, perfect can be BORING, not to mention exhausting. - :)

Chapter 6: Style is Planned

"Drawing a perfect eyebrow can be done without stencils. Simply use short, light strokes beginning inside and moving out, then returning and filling in as needed with a continuation of short strokes. The results, a natural look."

Angela Scott

"The more, the merrier!" doesn't necessarily apply to a real fashionista. *Quality* always outranks *quantity*. By quality, I don't necessarily mean the fabric quality. It's more about how valuable a piece of garment is to your style. It's about a piece's versatility and how it makes you look and feel.

Line up ten fashion-savvy women and ask them about their style and each will clearly articulate what their style profile is. They will also make no qualm about being deliberate in their style choices. This is because they have trained their eye for item selections that scream "me!". Getting dressed is like planning a trip -- it calls for some foresight; a road map, if you will. This starts with *your* intentions and goals. So I ask you, what are they?

You may be at a place in your life where you haven't quite figured out who you are (visit Chapter 1) or you know who you are but your personal style needs a lot of work (visit Chapter 5). Don't fret, in this chapter we will discuss fashion must-have staples that are affordable and fail-proof.

- Cozy knots
- Boyfriend blazer
- Ballet flats
- Little Black Dress (LBD)
- Bangles
- Black bag
- Metal watch
- Scarf
- White button-down shirt
- Black slacks

These wardrobe building blocks offer all you need to later personalize (yes, plan) your personal style.

Let's say two ladies, Jane and Shandra, work at the same firm. Shandra's style is impeccable. Janet covets Shandra's style, but Janet is not doing what it takes to reflect her own personal style. Wake up, Janet! Get up and do something!

Here's what to do for starters:

1. Start borrowing clothes & accessories from your friends: experiment & find out what works for you.
2. Start taking daily outfit photos.
3. Create yourself a rough style concept. (write it out)
4. Be prepared to spend some time thinking about your look.

Borrow from friends/ relatives, etc.
I say borrow because it's cheap! There's no sense in buying something which you're not sure about. A short-term loan from a friend/relative is a great way to discover what suits you and if you don't like it, just give it back but please, maintain it! (Maybe you could bribe them if there is something special you really like.) Allow them to dress you up if they're game; you never know, they just might hook you up in something you adore. Again, if you all are game, fill a plastic bag with accessories that they no longer wear; take them home and work them into your outfits over the next couple of weeks. Do you look better in small, sunglasses or huge, oversized shades? Are you more

comfortable with an enormous vintage doctor's bag or a clutch? You get the idea.

Start taking daily outfit photos
I cannot stress this enough. Do it with a Polaroid camera if you can. Stick them in the back of your Moleskine. Write commentary alongside each one, including what was good, what wasn't, and what you would change if you wore it again. This will make such a difference in the way you dress yourself and this will teach you a lot about your coloring, shape and proportions.

Create
For example: It doesn't need to be long, but flagrant use of adjectives can help solidify a picture in your head. You could start off simple, with *"wide-leg pants & cropped cardigans"*...but then expand it to *"wear with brooch & pearls"*. Allow your imagination to roam, and if all else fails, go back to step four!

Seriously, spend some quality time thinking about your look
The most stylish people do not magically conjure their outfits into existence; a lot of the time, their wardrobe is the cumulative effect of lots of list making, hunting, haggling and a staunch attitude towards keeping weird old treasures. Feel free to make mistakes because, if you're not making mistakes, you're not pushing the envelope hard enough. Finally, don't be afraid to redefine your style concept in an effort to make it wilder or more wearable. This will keep you from getting stale. Most importantly, remember, to

leave the house "undone" is a serious social misdemeanor.

When putting together a look, think about the adjectives that come to your mind when you think of what you want to project. "Strong", "elegant", "romantic", "perfectionist", "complex", "powerful", "capable", "sexy", "soft", "ambitious", "creative", "mysterious", "serious", and so on.

In my line of work, I often help clients put together "looks" and I always ask them how they would like to be perceived (both in general and for events). It may be important to look soft on a first date but powerful during the upcoming conference. No one who wants to look powerful for a conference dons a frilly frock. This calls for a well-tailored and structured power suit with power heels to match.

Tips for Days 104-132:

Day 104:
A spritz is all you need. Guys want to be drawn in, not knocked out. A great choice would be Bond No.9 Brooklyn. It's light but also spicy with a blend of citrus, spice and wood.

Day 105:
Schedule your monthly wax appointment so it falls after your period. Things hurt less when estrogen levels are high. Really, this is true!

Day 106:
After conditioning, rinse your hair with COLD water to close the cuticle for smooth, shiny locks. Shiny hair looks healthier.

Day 107:
Want the whites of your eyes to look brighter? Apply navy blue eyeliner to your top lids. This will compliment your eyes and make them sparkle. Absolutely!!!

Day 108:
Before whacking off all of your hair, or going asymmetrical or trying a new color or asking for the Halle cut, first try many styles on for size; you can view online beforehand. Essence.com has a Makeover Magic that allows you to upload your own photo and "try on" different hair do's.

Day 109:
I have two words...MAC dazzle. If you don't have one in your arsenal, get one! Perfect for any night you wish to GLAM OUT. Pucker up ever so sweetly!

Day 110:
I swear by John Freida's Hair Serum for fly – away hair. It's light and it does the job. For those of you who have hair that explodes into an uncontrollable bush as soon as the wind or rain heads in your direction, then this is the hair serum for you, keeping your hair straighter and for a longer timeframe. Remember... BIG hair, not BUSHY hair, is in for fall.

Day 111:
Like longer hems? The secret is to look for skirts that hit somewhere between or right below the knee down to mid-calf range. This will help keep proportions in check.

Day 112:
If you just want to even out your skin, MAC Prep + Prime Transparent Finishing Powder is fantastic because you can use it over moisturized or primed skin and look a little more put together, without having to apply foundation. I use it on top of my concealer and LOVE it! Also, if you apply a very bright blush, a little bit of this dusted over will subdue the color nicely, and, I might add….it's great for blush mishaps!

Day 113:
Delicate under-eye skin is probably the first place you will notice fine lines and wrinkles. In your 20's you

should already be in defense mode, combating the issue with an eye cream regimen. Do not skimp this step or it will surely show later!

Day 114:
MAC brushes. The next time their mini-brushes go on sale for $49.95, be sure to pick them up because that price is close to what you would normally pay for one brush! Precise application guaranteed.

Day 115:
To achieve a pop of color on your cheeks start by using two shades of blush. Apply your natural color and then add a pop of a brighter color on top. The natural shade looks great at first but often fades out quickly. The brighter shade alone is often great for evening but too much of a contrast for every day. This layering technique offers natural brightness. Simply put, beautiful!

Day 116:
Sephora sells a convenient brush cleaning spray for your makeup brushes. It's important to sanitize your brushes regularly between uses. Simply spray brushes used and then swipe with a paper towel....and it's sanitized, it's done! Fini!

Day 117:
Hoops are classic and every fashionista has them in her arsenal. Scale hoops to the size of your face. Thinner hoops look best on fine-boned, smaller faces, as they do not overwhelm the size of the face. Medium

to thick hoops compliment wide, full and/or strong face shapes.

Day 118:
The season's changing...Long-wear lip color or gloss lasts even longer on smooth lips. You can exfoliate your lips by slowly, gently brushing them with a toothbrush. But... if that does not appeal to you, LUSH sells a lip scrub (i.e., Sweet Lips, Mint Julips); or why not make your own lip scrub! Simply use olive oil and a dab of brown sugar to exfoliate; slowly, gently sloughs away. Either way, smooth is nice.

Day 119: Have a man?
Men, look like a million bucks and attract it. Your suits should never be worn "off the rack" no matter how well you "think" it fits. A tailor will do wonders for you.

Day 120:
Know where you are going and then DRESS the part.

Day 121:
Wear light and bright colors near your face. This draws the eye upward and brings attention and light to your face. Think tops, scarves, dresses, and jewelry.

Day 122:
Maybelline Define-A-Lash Waterproof Mascara will thicken and darken even the lightest of lashes and it will last through the *teariest* of movies and toasts.

Day 123:
Using MAC's bare canvas paint on lids prior to eye shadow will make your eyes look bigger, not to mention "wow".

Day 124:
Cutting your hair can be liberating, true, when you need a change. However, you'll be sure to turn heads if cut right. Hence, seek a stylist with a reputable rap sheet. Don't cut corners.

Day 125:
Don a faux fur scarf or faux fur cropped jacket for fall. Tres chic!

Day 126:
You don't need 100 cheap handbags. Invest in and maintain 3-4 NICE ones. They will instantly upgrade anything else you are rocking. Trust me!

Day 127:
False lashes can look great yet they can be cumbersome... not to mention most ladies who wear them abuse them (i.e., wearing them too long, sleeping in them) which irritates the eyes and can lead to infection. If false eye lashes are not your thing opt for a lash primer! Best of both worlds!

Day 128:
It doesn't have to match, it just has to go.

Day 129:
Oil of Olay's exfoliation system is incredible. It makes a huge difference in my makeup applications. Don't have a system, get one!

Day 130:
Got nice legs? Of course you do! Don tights, boots and... SHORTS! Especially loving the cable knit sweater/ turtleneck/ BLING/ shorts/ tights/ heels/ boots look!

Day 131:
Pieces with versatility will keep your closet clutter-free.

Day 132:
Ladies! I'm on this versatility kick. Invest in an eye shadow compact and you can go from day to night with ease!

Chapter 7: A Tribute to French Swagger

"By far, the most attractive and powerful style accessory you can have is a vision. Take the time to do your inner self-work, focus on making your vision a reality, and spend time in the presence of the Lord and you will turn heads wherever you go."

Ericka D. Jackson

Are you admiring the shoe on the cover of this book? Who can fault you? It was chosen as a tribute to French swagger. It was designed by Mai Lamore, French-speaking, haute-couture shoe designer born in Central Africa. Sent to France by her parents to complete her studies, she was immersed in the world of fashion and art. In an interview for the UK edition of Vogue, the French shoe designer, Mai Lamore, explains the concept behind any of her shoes: "A shoe, more than any other clothing item, is an object that already exists before even being worn; shoes do not generally fold up or fall lifeless as most clothing items do when not worn. This 'object' quality has a certain mystery to it, akin to a sculpture with a life of its own. A high luxury shoe should look as stunning on the foot as it would in a *vitrine* [window]."

Mai Lamore's $27,945 rose shoe has a 14K covered sculptured stiletto with hand-dyed silk rose petals at the heel.

(Yes, I did say $27,945.). These breath-taking shoes were discovered in a 2007 issue of Elite Traveler. Parisian shoe designer Mai Lamore has successfully mastered the blending of art with shoe design. Her works of art are nowadays known globally for their artistic feature (couture) which transforms a shoe into a *statement*. Mai Lamore shoes feature precious stones, feathers, bejeweled platforms, slinky panther, leopard sandals, golden heels, and silk petals. Wow! The woman is inspiring. I love that she is influenced by African and French cultures. Somehow I cannot help but feel very connected to her despite never meeting her. I love her French swagger.

Why the affinity to French? I had the awesome opportunity of living in Europe for nine years, six of those years in Belgique. I speak French and love to meet people who share the language and culture. While there, I enjoyed the Belgian cuisine, the cobble-stone roads downtown and the cathedral-styled buildings laced with intricate detail. I loved the smell of bread baking at the B*oulangerie* and the cute cars that took up so little space. I truly miss the style sense; I remember how I would frequent the local boutiques that had all the lovely, lady-like gloves and dainty purses and sweet-smelling fragrances. I miss how every year I traveled to Paris and basked in the scents of cafes and the sight of streets filled with artists in open-air exhibitions and its luxurious appeal. One could say that French is engrained in me.

Then, there is a certain *"je ne sais quoi"* about French women. "*Less is more*" is the philosophy French women are well known to uphold. The French have been the pioneers of chic fashion for hundreds of years. From Chanel to Givenchy, they all share the same vision: Smart, timeless, sophisticated yet feminine style! Is it because French women are more interested in having a life than merely making a living? Is it because they don't covet packaged cookie-cutter beauty? Is it because *less is more* in France? You decide. All I know is that there is a certain confidence and *"je ne sais quoi"* about French women that is indeed, very admirable.

Tips for Days 133-151:

Day 133:
Aveeno's Soothing Bath for dry, winter skin. Miracle worker.

Day 134:
If you have thin lips choose light-to-medium lip color shades and avoid dark shades, they have a minimizing effect.

Day 135:
Fill in sparse areas or holes in your brows with a creamy eye pencil. For the most natural look, layer powder shadow on top.

Day 136:
Ladies... Moisturize the delicate skin around the eyes with a lightweight eye cream to ensure under-eye concealer goes on smoothly and evenly.

Day 137:
A pointed-toe stiletto will always make your legs appear longer and leaner than a rounded toe. So, what's a girl to do when rounded toes are making a pretty serious comeback? Opt for the pointier round-toe shoes (forgo the super-round-toes altogether; say this with me again...ALTOGETHER). If you are slightly "vertically challenged" opt for the pointier round-toe platform.

Day 138:
Have short or sparse lashes and tired of the dreaded routine that comes with falsies? Consider Revlon's Grown Luscious Fabulash Mascara. In a rent study, 96% of participants saw marked growth. By next summer, your batting average may just put you on the map.

Day 139:
Lip products 101: When it comes to lip stains, dab on the lip balm and blend quickly because they dry pretty fast. When it comes to mattes, use a bit of conditioning balm allowing it to sink in fully before applying your matte stick; As for creams, they rub off easily so be sure to prep the entire surface with liner first. Glosses require no prep, offering just a hint of color and lots of shine. When choosing lip apps keep these things in mind. I LOVE A CREAM STICK over (on top of) gloss. Today I'm wearing Bobbi Brown's Baby Peach lipstick over Bobbi Brown's Nude Gloss paired with my Smoky eyes from Bobbi Brown's holiday collection "Day to Night Warm Eye Palette" It is absolutely GORGEOUS!!!

Day 140:
Just say no to Christmas sweaters in the office. (With my finger down my throat, I'm pleading with you...) Just don't! Frosty's playing a quick game of peek-a-boo with this tacky Christmas sweater, emerging from the button to say hello.

Day 141:
Wear underwear that is near your skin tone. There will be those times that you have to wear white and the fabric may not be that thick. So buy a bra, thong and bikini panties in a shade closest to your skin tone.

Day 142:
Make putting on your makeup a beautiful experience, not an afterthought. Allowing a bit of extra time for pre-party primping can get you into a sexier state of mind - and keep you from looking like you just threw your makeup on last minute.

To do: Plan out what makeup you intend to wear well in advance of a bash, much like you would your outfit. On the day of the event, cleanse and moisturize before applying your makeup and be sure to sweep on setting powder to give your look staying power. And don't forget to toss a shimmer powder into your bag for touch-ups.

Day 143:
For natural looking definition and to keep color from feathering, line lips with lip liner AFTER applying lip color. Use the lip brush to soften and blend any hard edges.

Day 144:
Now that Winter is nigh, rub a light layer of Vaseline onto your cuticles before retiring for the night; this will keep them supple and crack-free.

Day 145:
When rushing to put away clothing in your closet, you may fail to pay much attention to where you are placing certain items. Be sure to place light-colored garments out of range of dyed denims that can rub off on and stain pale clothing. White jeans, for example, are best placed in between your khaki slacks --not in between your dark denim skinny jeans.

Day 146:
When you moisturize your face, moisturize your neck as well. A smooth firm face next to a wrinkled neck... not so cute. Also, be sure to use a heavier cream for winter months. Clinique's hydration formula is fab!

Day 147:
Invest in several versatile outfits that can go from work to date with a simple change in shoes, makeup and accessories. This is the best reason to invest in dresses. I love a dress for its functionality and style. Added panache...the right one can be quite slimming!

Day 148:
Sleep on satin or silk pillow cases; doing so will create fewer creases on your face and delays the onset of wrinkles.

Day 149:
Very of the moment, adding "bling-shock" to your dress-down outfit will give you both that instant pop you crave alongside the laid-back comfort you relish in. I'm thinking sequins and cotton this weekend. What about you?

Day 150:
So now, I ask you, "What is your feature?" Whatever it is, play it up. Blending in, well, it's so passé.

Day 151:
Going to a holiday party? Glitter up your manicure; paint a double layer of posh gold lacquer on fingers and toes. Try Chanel's Gold Fiction. Or try the foils; this posh color lasts only a few days – so you can save for special occasions.

Chapter 8: Exclamation Points!!!

"For those of us who have been blessed to be of the dark chocolate complexion - don't be afraid of those bright, vibrant colors! Shades like lime green, golden yellow and yes, even hot pink look fabulous on our skin!"

Darlene Thorne

"Ladies, if you keep a small tube of Vaseline with you in your purse daily, this can serve as a beauty enhancement life saver. A small dab on your lips, a little around your cuticles, and a small amount rubbed on your heels in between pedicures will help you to stay poised and polished for any occasion."

Judy W. Farr

Finishing touches polish your look. These no-no's can quickly turn a style Diva into a style disaster.

Visible Panty lines
A huge no-no. Why? They disrupt the clean line that is a must in any silhouette. Not to mention they draw unsightly attention to the backside. Not attractive. The thong is a life-saver.

Visible Muffin-tops
The bulging makes you look bigger than you are and breaks the line that is a must in any silhouette. Don high-waist jeans and opt instead for a Spanx with smooth lines.

Scuffed sneakers
Unless exercising, there is nothing feminine about grass-stained sneakers at the local market. Ugh! Flat boots, sandals and ballet flats can be just as comfortable.

Shapeless t-shirt
Save them for spring cleaning where you cannot be seen. They do nothing for a woman's silhouette but enlarge it. Opt for slimming cuts with ruching on the sides and lower necklines.

Abundance of skin
Excess cleavage and leg will get you glances but not the promotion you are hoping for.

Travel in style
Okay, you have a six hour flight? It is understandable you want to be comfortable, but don't take comfort too far. Leave the scuffed sneakers, bandana/head scarf and/or sweats at home. No embarrassing run-ins to worry about. Besides, you are still representing your company (especially if you manage/own it).

Befriend your tailor
Here is not the place to be stingy. Tailoring is everything in fit. It gives the polish that distinguishes an off-the-rack from a custom.

Tips for Days 152-170:

Day 152:
Primer Time! Here's the skinny. Putting on primer can save you major effort. Wear it solo to look flawless without foundation or use it under makeup to help your coverage last longer. Hint: If you have oily skin, look for a silicone on the label to mute shine. This is what I use. If you have dry skin, look for a glycerin formula for firming and hydration.

Day 153:
Perfume on wrists should be dabbed or fanned, never rubbed. Otherwise it loses its truth.

Day 154:
Did you know that working in an aesthetically pleasant environment impacts our attitudes, well so does being around aesthetically pleasing people. If your game is not tight, get it tight because if you don't invest in you, no one else will.

Quote of the Day: "I have been expressing myself with clothes since I was a kid-- I can convey my emotions much better that way."
Hamish Bowles

Day 155: Have a man?
Men with bald heads who shave constantly to maintain their look must exfoliate their heads! This can even be done with sugar and lotion prior to a shave. Rinse and follow with moisturizing products that

contain Aloe Vera. Result........smooth, radiant sex appeal. (Take Note: razor bumps, not so sexy).

Day 156:
Baths are so soothing but can be so drying for your skin. This winter try adding a few drops of baby oil to enhance your indulgence and use a loofah.

Day 157:
It's better to have 10 outfits that make you look (and feel) like you are on top of your game (A class) than a closet full of cheap clothes that make you feel C class. 90% classic, 10% fad.

Day 158:
Make sure your wardrobe reflects your vision. People see you before they know you.

Day 159:
Black on black looks best when the textures are mixed. Leather with lace, taffeta with chiffon, suede with cotton... You get the point. So, when going for monochromatic, play on texture to avoid looking "dated" and uninteresting.

Day 160:
Remember, panty hose before jewelry; pullovers before makeup.

Day 161:
Employ your fingers to warm your concealer, to blend your foundation and mix lip shades together;

even work makeup into the face for seamlessness. It's all about the warmth of those fingertips.

Day 162:
You just ran your $10 pantyhose. Don't trash them; keep those to wear under leggings to give you smoother lines. Add knee-high boots and it's a wrap.

Day 163:
Business: Scan receipts for any new clothing you purchase for your transition. Eight receipts per page does the trick! Happy shopping!

Day 164:
Don't wear gloves to wash the dishes like mama? Keep a nice hand lotion pump beside your kitchen sink. The next time you finish the dishes you will immediately reach to moisturize your hands, and hence, your cuticles. The average wait time can takes its toll, leading to prematurely aged hands. Rub a dub dub!

Day 165:
Style changes everything.

Day 166:
Check out what next season is all about (bold colors, textures, prints etc…). That way you can ease it into your closet now!

Day 167:
Your play on novelty patterns and stripes must be intentional, your tie-in should be fluid.

Day 168:
Formal dresses can always be toned down for less-than-formal events with a blazer (think suede, corduroy, tweed, denim even). What we love about the typical formal is its slimming effect. Eyes keep on following the line.

Day 169:
Be confident in your style of dress. The dress doesn't wear you; you wear the dress.

Day 170:
Keep your nails neutral for interviews. All focus should be on you.

Day 171:
Become a label sleuth before you are "had". Counterfeiters neglect details-often using the wrong font, making spelling mistakes, using inferior materials and shoddy workmanship.

Commentary: Divas Let Loose

Many thanks to my contributors!
Each is a woman leader impacting her flock.

Shekina Moore
Designer. Stylist. Entrepreneur. Author.

www.SoKinaOnline.com

"Perhaps you tend to avoid stepping outside of your comfort zone and just keep it safe. However doing that only keeps you away from fully developing your sense of style and it results in feeling like your style is boring."

~Divas Let Loose~

Marshawn Evans
Author. Speaker. Attorney.

www.MarshawnEvans.com

"At the end of each dry hot summer day, HYDRATE your skin. Use a soft facial cleanser, follow up with a toner; apply a serum designed for your skin type, and finish with a night moisturizer to wake up refreshed and renewed."

"S.T.Y.L.E. (Show That You Live Excellence) Style should reflect your personal brand. Accessories are the best tools to accentuate your style. Whether it's a flower in your hair or on your lapel, be bold and be elegant. Most importantly, be YOU."

~Divas Let Loose~

Tanea Smith
Owner, She's Got Papers

www.shesgotpapers.com

"Nothing says power & confidence like a signature color. Find the hue that brings your spirit to life and work it!"

~Divas Let Loose~

Denise Tunnell
Celebrity Makeup Artist.

www.denisetunnell.com

"Create a tinted moisturizer for sheer coverage by mixing your foundation with a sunscreen or your favorite moisturizer."

"Maintain a groomed eyebrow to elevate your look."

~Divas Let Loose~

Barbara Hemphill
Organizational Expert.
Owner Productive Environment Institute

www.productiveenvironment.com

"Consider ways you can incorporate your brand into wardrobe -- with your logo, a recognizable piece of jewelry, or a specific color. For years I was known as the "Paper Tiger Lady' and my wardrobe was full of tiger stripes which was fun and memorable for my clients!"

~Divas Let Loose~

Angela Scott
Author. Pastor.

www.bornagainministries.org

"Drawing a perfect eyebrow can be done without stencils. Simply use short, light strokes beginning inside and moving out, then returning and filling in as needed with a continuation of short strokes. The results: a natural look."

~Divas Let Loose~

Ericka D. Jackson
President, The Convergence Center LLC

www.erickajackson.com

"By far, the most attractive and powerful style accessory you can have is a vision. Take the time to do your inner self-work, focus on making your vision a reality, and spend time in the presence of the Lord and you will turn heads wherever you go."

~Divas Let Loose~

Darlene Thorne
Author. Founder; A Heart After the Father Ministries

www.darlenethorne.com

"For those of us who have been blessed to be of the dark chocolate complexion - don't be afraid of those bright vibrant colors! Shades like lime green, golden yellow and yes, even hot pink look fabulous on our skin!"

~Divas Let Loose~

Judy W. Farr
Evangelist. Speaker. Entrepreneur.

www.judyfarr.com

"Ladies, keeping a small tube of Vaseline with you in your purse can serve as a beauty enhancement life saver. A small tab on your lips, a little around your cuticles, a small amount rubbed on your heels in between pedicures will help you to stay poised and polished for any occasion."

~Divas Let Loose~

Nadia Shirin Moffett
Miss North Carolina USA 2010.
Executive Director, The Queen's Foundation, Inc.

www.thequeensfoundation.org

"The right heels bring elegance to any outfit -- To ensure your feet aren't in pain all day, always be less conservative when choosing a size. Go up half a size to give your feet room to breathe, so you can walk hard in your pumps! "

Less glam is more! Too often we are wearing too much glam in one outfit. Its messy and looks like we're trying too hard. An elegant look philosophy is this: pick one item to be your centerpiece to the outfit and everything else in the outfit is a compliment. Is it a splash of color in the shoes, glam earrings or chunky necklace? Pick one item to make your outfit unique yet sophisticated.

Call It A Cheat Sheet

Tip of the Day:
If you want to create a slimmer waist accessorize with a waist belt. This is an easy way to create more shape in your silhouette.

Tip of the Day:
Are you confined to Blacks and Grays? Spice up your wardrobe. Add a splash of color here and there.

Tip of the Day:
When wearing knee length dresses or skirts, or even shorter, why not make it pop with a pair of stiletto pumps? Accentuate those fabulous legs.

Tip of the Day:
Don't be afraid to accessorize. Accessories are key to coordination. You can go flashy with long, dangled earrings and purse or play it simple with a scarf and a nice pair of studded earrings.

Tip of the Day:
Remember you walk your own red carpet every day. You have to be comfortable in what you wear. Choose apparel that compliments your natural silhouette.

Tip of the Day:
What do you like best about yourself? Expose the beauty of you. Nice legs? Try a split! Lovely shoulders or a lovely back? Rock those halters and backless

tops. If you really want to show off, go low in a plunged neckline. Be tasteful in whatever you wear.

Tip of the Day:
What is your style? Are you simple and elegant or an eccentric Diva? Let your character shine through!

Tip of the Day:
Keep Visine Tears handy for times when you have overdone it, or when you are worn/burned out, especially when you still have to LOOK put together nonetheless. Never let 'em see you sweat.

Tip of the Day:
Ladies, we have all experienced sucking the tummy in for pictures. If your dress hugs all those "curves", slip on a body shaper. You want to be ready for any unexpected photo shoot. The cameras are always rolling.

Tip of the Day:
For long lasting, glamorous lashes, apply them individually, avoiding direct eye contact with water.

Tip of the Day:
Bangles in natural textures or bright hues are big for spring. Whatever your style, pile them on for maximum effect.

Tip of the Day:
Play up off the shoulder/V-neck blouses with a turtleneck underneath.

Tip of the Day:
Removing makeup with a facial cleanser promotes healthy skin.

Tip of the Day:
If you do not normally wear foundation, but still want coverage, try a mineral powder. Powders are lightweight and easily removed. You can always get your color matched at local makeup counters.

Tip of the Day:
If you have a special evening planned, make sure you base your lips with a balm prior to gloss/lipstick. This prevents premature chapping and promotes longer wear of lip applicators.

Tip of the Day:
If you want to create the illusion of longer legs, pump it up! Pumps and stilettos create the look of longer legs. Higher the heels, longer the legs.

Tip of the Day:
A one-piece is a simple ensemble to put together. For those who are heavier in the hips, tummy or bust line draped fabric does well in camouflaging those areas.

Tip of the Day:
Cocktail dresses are a great way to flaunt your shape for an outing. This is for both curvy hips and not so curvy hips. Classy, chic and elegant.

Tip of the Day:
Eventually, spring time will roll around again, so, time to start looking at flowing dresses and open toed shoes. What will your wardrobe be like?

Tip of the Day:
Dusting your back and shoulders with body shimmer gives an eye-catching glow for those evenings out.

Tip of the Day:
For added support in backless or low neck lines, try an adhesive bra. If you have a dropped neck line get the adhesive strips that go under the bust line. These also create the same lifted effect.

Tip of the Day:
Sometimes when wearing flared skirts, a lot can be seen underneath. To prevent over-exposure in flared dresses/skirts, go for a length at least three inches above the knees or longer.

Tip of the Day:
When wearing your shoulders out make sure the cut is high under the arms to avoid bulging and bra exposure.

Tip of the Day:
If you are shy about your arms, three quarter-length sleeves are perfect for covering them up.

Tip of the Day:
It's important that you keep your skin well moisturized. This preserves your skin from premature aging.

Tip of the Day:
It's always good to pack a back up. Just in case.

Tip of the Day:
Accessories go further than just earrings and bangles. You can accessorize your hair as well. Try beaded headbands for added flare.

Tip of the Day:
When in need of a touch up, keep a makeup bag in your purse. This creates easy access for those needed touch-ups.

Tip of the Day:
If you are looking to have added support in your swimsuit, try wide straps or underwire.

Tip of the Day:
Dresses with pockets create the illusion of curves. If you already have them, pockets will accentuate them.

Tip of the Day:
If you are concerned about your cleavage being exposed, camis are a fashionable way to cover up. Purchase them in colors that can be easily coordinated.

Tip of the Day:
Undergarments are an important part of your wardrobe. Neutral colors hide well in transparent fabric. If you have a dark skin tone, black hides better.

Tip of the Day:
Nail polish is a great way to show your personality. Short nails do best.

Tip of the Day:
Quality denim is a must. You want to keep them for a while without shrinkage. Keep in mind, good jeans last forever and never go out of style.

Tip of the Day:
It's best to use white cloth when cleansing your face. Dyes from a colored cloth can transfer to your pores. This can cause uneven pigmentation.

Tip of the Day:
Our hair style can make or break our ensemble. Up do's are very elegant. Go chic with a wild frenzied curl.

Tip of the Day:
For a comfortable fit with flare, gaucho pants are perfect. These can easily be dressed up with a high pump or dressed down with a sandal.

Tip of the Day:
If you want to take a subtle approach with a strappy shoe, go with a nude or a natural color.

Tip of the Day:
Lace is an elegant way of staying cool and classy. Easily dressed up or down.

Tip of the Day:
Jeans are a comfortable classic. Dress them up with a form shaping jacket. Canvas/leather materials give a clean sophisticated look. For women in a casual setting, a peep toe shoe would be perfect. Guys, a dress shoe with similar jacket texture would work well.

Tip of the Day:
A printed shoe can easily be dressed up. Prints are eye-catching so simple accessories and neutral tones will help keep your shoe the focal point.

Tip of the Day:
Wide leg bottoms give your body proportion. Not recommended for short legs.

Tip of the Day:
The color orange made a bold statement this year. This vibrant color easily compliments all skin tones. Get hip to spring's bright color schemes and add excitement to your wardrobe.

Tip of the Day:
A skinny belt defines your waistline when worn with loose fits and flowing fabrics.

Tip of the Day:
Why not YOU? Same lipstick shade you were wearing in 1989? Same shade of polish for the past two

months/two years/decade? Same weight goal you had last year? Same haircut you rocked in high school? If you've been stuck in a rut, try something NEW. Up the glam quotient! Your best years are now in sight.

Tip of the Day:
ORANGE LIPS. What better accessory to TAUPE or GRAY attire then a sheer orange pout? Lighter skin tones should try a coral-pink orange; deeper tones a tomato orange; golden-olive tones a bright orange! PAH-DOW!!!

Tip of the Day:
Want radiant legs, back, arms, shoulders, and feet? Add Vaseline oil-gel to your FAV scented lotion. The look/sniff combination is lethal.

Tip of the Day:
When people in your environment are dressing beneath your standard, always keep in perspective that you dress for where you are going. In essence, for what you are called to, not for where you are and who you just happen to be around.

Tip of the Day:
Have a hard time accepting compliments? Never play down a compliment. Gracefully accept it. Avoid phrases like "Oh, these old things?"; "You think so?"; "No, I'm not!"; "Don't let the look fool you, I got them for $5.99 on clearance." These answers are negative in nature and usually turn into awkward conversations that make the person who complimented you second-

guess their compliment, and they might not compliment you again. Really! So, repeat after me: "Thank you!"....... Now, was that so hard?

Tip of the Day:
Dressing for success includes more than just choosing the right outfit. For a professional look, always consider accessories and personal grooming. A man's/woman's professional appearance needs to support his/her professional accomplishments. If your business attire is distracting because it is too sexy, drab, or colorful, business contacts may focus on how you look, not your business skills.

Tip of the Day:
Going out to run a few errands? Or maybe heading to the grocery store or the dry cleaners? Don't just throw on anything; take time to make yourself look presentable. You never know who you're going to run into or what you are going to encounter. Remember...someone is ALWAYS watching.

Tip of the Day:
"Oops! I forgot to..." Don't let this become your "signature phrase". Get organized! A well-organized person always proves to be less stressed and less tense. When your time is organized, so is your mind. When your mind is organized you are able to be a more relaxed you, and productive. Be your best self by planning ahead and avoid the unattractiveness of disorganization!

Tip of the Day:
Consider this when going to purchase a new handbag
1. Black or brown leather bags are essential & can be worn with almost anything.
2. Cross-body bags are comfortable and perfect for on the go.
3. A Clutch is a MUST HAVE in every woman's wardrobe. It just fits!
Remember: Let your personality show when choosing your bag. This accessory says more about you than you may think.

Tip of the Day:
When shopping for new clothes, never shop for a certain size. Instead, always shop for the RIGHT SIZE. This means you may have to actually try on your clothes before you leave the store. This helps to avoid purchasing the wrong size for your body type. Remember: *RIGHT SIZE* not *CERTAIN SIZE*!

Tip of the Day:
One very important thing to keep in mind when getting ready to go out is to give yourself enough time. There's nothing worse than having to rush getting ready only to forget something or see that you aren't as well put together as you'd like to be. To avoid this, plan ahead. Begin the process early enough so that you can take your time to look your best no matter where you're going!

Tip of the Day:
Looking to add some color to your wardrobe? Step out of the box and incorporate colorful bottoms! Pants are usually neutral, so when worn in a bright color, they quickly become the center of attention and the key item in the outfit. Start with something subtle; pair your bright colored trousers with softer colors and low-key pieces like a classic white shirt or brown leather shoulder bags. If pear-shaped, keep bottoms on darker spectrum and opt for color up top.

Tip of the Day:
Need a good makeup remover? Try Neutrogena's Makeup Remover Cleansing Towelettes.

Woman of the Day:
Billie Holiday - Rouse the crowd like Billie Holiday with soulful lounge wear, slinky tops, and songbird feather touches!!

Tip of the Day:
For the mom who cares for fashion, there is a great selection of gifts you can get her for Mother's Day. Choose stylish designed handbags, intricate, one-of-a-kind accessories or even a cute pair of shoes. The options are limitless!! Make mom feel special by going out of your way to find something that fits her perfectly and will remind her of how fearfully and wonderfully she's made!!

Tip of the Day:
Every lady needs a statement piece of jewelry that you absolutely love. If you have just one piece, you

obviously can't wear it all the time, but when you do wear it, it upgrades the outfit tenfold. It's that piece that people always comment on and makes you feel fashionable from the moment you put it on.

Tip of the Day:
Need a little help picking out the correct undergarments? Here are a few tips: If the band rides up your back the bra is too small. If the cups don't fit and your twins are falling out of the bra, you need to up the cup size and wear the right size bra. Eliminate any visible panty lines in your clothing. Choose boy shorts in a microfiber or thin mesh fabric to conceal your panty lines. When in doubt, *thongs* will work wonders.

Tip of the Day:
Before we know it, the heat and humidity will be here again real soon. Heat and humidity have taken over. Here are a few tips to keep you cool during your work day: Layering helps with commutes in hot weather. When done right, you can remove layers throughout the day. Try doing your hair in an up do or pulled back before you leave the house. Lastly, choose your fabrics wisely. Linens and light cottons will help you to avoid overheating.

Tip of the Day:
If your legs are a little shorter, or you just want your legs to look longer, stay away from ankle straps. Ankle straps cut off right at the ankle, making your legs appear shorter. Now if you're fine with the way your legs look, by all means go right ahead!

To get the appearance of longer legs, try either stiletto, pumps, or even small heeled sandals; they will make the legs look great as they thin them out.

Tip of the Day: Have a man?
For the professional man just starting his wardrobe, I recommend beginning with a dark suit, whether black, navy, charcoal or grey. Build around it with shirts, ties and sport coats. Once the basics are established, it is then safe to start expanding with lighter shades such as khakis, taupes and browns. My professional advice is to overdress rather than under dress for any business affair

Tip of the Day:
Men with significant others, do not be shy telling your woman she looks and smells good. When she comes home with a new 'do, it would be wise to acknowledge and compliment her. Believe us! If you are not... plenty of men on the street, on the job, in the market place will. Let's keep it tight this year as she keeps her game tight. Show those watching how it is done.

Tip of the Day:
Closed-toe stilettos keep things from looking too casual. This is precisely why they pair nicely with cool sunglasses, cable-knit sweaters and patterned skirts for fall.

Tip of the Day:
Add yellow to an outfit to make it much more fun. A great example is a plain white fitted tee, skinny jeans and nude heels with an oversized yellow clutch.

Tip of the Day:
Gladiator sandals are a way to be fashion forward but comfortable. They can be worn with skinny jeans to maxi dress.

Tip of the Day:
Leopard Print! It's a funky mix of neutral colors. The best way to wear this trend is one piece at a time or it will be too much. Try it out with a pair of leopard wedges for the summer and a leopard scarf for the winter.

Tip of the Day:
Black Nail Polish. During Summer months a lot of us are reaching for the bright colors, but did you know black nail polish protects your nails from the sun? It will always look classic yet edgy no matter the season so go ahead and try it.

Tip of the Day:
Be polite. Style isn't just about the clothes you wear but also how you present yourself and treat others. Hold the door open for someone when you get the chance or compliment someone's outfit.

Tip of the Day:
White button-down shirt and a black pencil skirt. This combination is classic and you can add your own personal touch to the outfit with shoes and accessories.

Tip of the Day:
Tie a silk scarf around your purse handle. It can update an old purse and add a unique touch to a plain bag.

Tip of the Day:
Sequins: They are eye-catching and will get you noticed. Great to spice up your night out.

Tip of the Day:
Wear a flower or vintage feather in your hair. Try it in a bright color. It's unique and unexpected.

Tip of the Day:
Smile. Your smile is one of the best accessories that you have naturally. It will put you and everyone that you come in contact with in a good mood. Nothing is more stylish than that.

Biography

Shekina Moore has been in North Carolina most of her life but had the awesome experience of living in Europe for nine years. She is very thankful to her parents for exposing her to European culture because while in Europe she took an affinity to French, absorbing the language, culture and undeniable fashion sense. The French have a way with fashion that she could not help but appreciate. It became a part of who she is and her style would never be the same. She has been creating and painting faces, framing brows, styling and wardrobing since the age of twelve.

In 1994, Shekina began to dabble with make-up and fashion trends. In college, her dormitory door had postings of her services along with pricing. Off-campus clientele were coming on campus to have her do their hair and eyebrows and even pick out their "date-fits" [outfits for dates and events]. Consistently told she was gifted, she did not completely yield to that gift by way of trade. She didn't quite yet understand that her gift would make room for her. Through the years, she continued to dabble in makeup and fashion "on the side." However, in 2007 something clicked as clear as crystal: "Work in your calling!" She was seriously unfulfilled, grumpy even. She realized that it was only when she was working in her passion (that thing that drives you, the thing you think about before bed and wake up thinking about) that she was energized! Bringing out the beauty in someone gives her unparalleled, matchless pleasure and fulfillment.

Shekina has worked on the style team of the Step N2 College TV Show and hosted the Speedy Outfitters Show with Your Time TV Network. Having worked on about every skin tone, texture and body type in the past few years, Shekina's development as an artist has grown exponentially. Just as important, it has given her an appreciation for beauty in all packaging and helped Shekina to narrow her focus in the industry.

Today Shekina runs her own business, Speedy Outfitters LLC, doing what she loves and holds dear...STYLE. In honor of her affinity for the femininity of the dress, she launched her label *SoKINA* in Fall 2011. The dress collection is one made especially for women leaders looking to express their femininity and let their hair down. Shekina was named the "Featured Designer" of the Carolina Music Awards 2011. Equally impressive, this acclaimed Style Guru is a former school administrator and doctoral candidate at North Carolina State University and author of book and style guide *"Shoeing The Fat"* in 2011.

When Shekina is not mixing and matching or designing wardrobe pieces, she is surely speaking on or actively engaged in her calling [the winning combination of] entrepreneurship, education and style. In her down time, Shekina enjoys time with God (quintessential to her purpose in this life), fun times with family and friends, travel, reading and sipping on her favorite indulgence... vanilla chai tea!